EASY TAPAS COOKBOOK

From Patatas Bravas to Paella The 25 Unmissable Spanish Recipes For A True Culinary Fiesta

Emma Yang

© Copyright 2023 by Emma Yang - All rights reserved.

Without the prior written permission of the Publisher, no part of this publication may be stored in a retrieval system, replicated, or transferred in any form or medium, digital, scanning, recording, printing, mechanical, or otherwise, except as permitted under 1976 United States Copyright Act, section 107 or 108. Permission concerns should be directed to the publisher's permission department.
Legal Notice

This book is copyright protected. It is only to be used for personal purposes. Without the author's or publisher's permission, you cannot paraphrase, quote, copy, distribute, sell, or change any part of the information in this book.
Disclaimer Notice

This book is written and published independently. Please keep in mind that the material in this publication is solely for educational and entertaining purposes. All efforts have provided authentic, up-to-date, trustworthy, and comprehensive information. There are no express or implied assurances. The purpose of this book's material is to assist readers in having a better understanding of the subject matter. The activities, information, and exercises are provided solely for self-help information. This book is not intended to replace expert psychologists, legal, financial, or other guidance. If you require counseling, please get in touch with a qualified professional.

By reading this text, the reader accepts that the author will not be held liable for any damages, indirectly or directly, experienced due to the use of the information included herein, particularly, but not limited to, omissions, errors, or inaccuracies. You are accountable for your decisions, actions, and consequences as a reader.

PREFACE

Welcome to the world of Spanish cuisine, where the vibrant flavors, colorful ingredients, and convivial spirit of tapas reign supreme. In this chapter, we embark on a journey through the rich and diverse tapestry of Spanish gastronomy, exploring the art of tapas. Originating from the lively bars and bustling streets of Spain, tapas have become a culinary sensation around the globe, capturing the essence of Spanish culture, community, and culinary creativity.

The tradition of tapas traces its roots back to the colorful and vibrant regions of Spain. Legend has it that King Alfonso X, while recovering from an illness, ordered small bites of food to be served with his wine. This practice, intended to ward off the ill effects of alcohol, soon gained popularity and evolved into a culinary tradition that has since become synonymous with Spanish socializing and hospitality.

The word "tapas" itself comes from the Spanish verb "tapar," meaning "to cover." Initially, small slices of bread or meat were used to cover wine glasses to prevent fruit flies from buzzing around the sweet libations. Over time, these "covers" transformed into delectable bite-sized dishes served alongside drinks, creating a culture of shared plates and communal feasting.

Tapas embody the spirit of togetherness, fostering lively conversations, laughter, and a sense of camaraderie among friends, family, and even strangers. They are a celebration of Spain's rich culinary heritage and showcase the country's bountiful ingredients, regional specialties, and culinary creativity.

Traditionally, tapas were served as a prelude to a meal or as a social gathering with drinks. However, today, they have evolved into a culinary art form, offering a wide array of flavors, textures, and combinations that can be enjoyed as a standalone meal or as part of a larger dining experience.

One of the most captivating aspects of tapas is their incredible variety. From succulent meats and seafood to vibrant vegetables and bold spices, tapas encompass a diverse range of flavors and ingredients. Whether it's the sizzling gambas al ajillo, the creamy patatas bravas, or the tangy boquerones en vinagre, each tapa tells a unique story and offers a delightful culinary experience.

In this chapter, we will explore a curated collection of tapas recipes that capture the essence of Spanish cuisine. From the classics to modern interpretations, each recipe is designed to transport you to the sun-drenched streets of Spain, where the aroma of spices fills the air and the clinking of glasses mingles with laughter.

So, join us on this culinary adventure as we dive into the world of tapas, exploring the flavors, techniques, and traditions that make them an integral part of Spanish culture. From traditional taverns to modern gastrobars, tapas continue to bring people together, inviting us to savor the vibrant tapestry of flavors that define Spanish gastronomy. ¡Buen provecho!

TRADITIONAL FOOD

These eight fundamental traditional Spanish foods showcase the rich culinary heritage and diverse regional flavors that define Spanish cuisine. Each dish carries with it a piece of history, reflecting the cultural traditions, local ingredients, and culinary ingenuity of the Spanish people.

Paella
A beloved Spanish dish, paella originated in the region of Valencia. This rice-based dish is traditionally cooked in a wide, shallow pan and combines a variety of ingredients such as saffron, rice, chicken, rabbit, vegetables, and seafood. Its roots can be traced back to the 18th century, where it was traditionally cooked by farmers and laborers over an open fire in the fields.

Jamón Ibérico
Considered the pinnacle of Spanish cured meats, Jamón Ibérico is made from the meat of the black Iberian pig. These pigs are reared in specific regions of Spain and fed on acorns, resulting in rich and flavorful meat. The curing process can take up to three years, with the ham being carefully aged in cellars. Jamón Ibérico has a long-standing tradition in Spain, with a history dating back centuries.

Tortilla Española
This iconic Spanish omelette is a staple in households across the country. Made from simple ingredients such as eggs, potatoes, onions, and olive oil, the tortilla is cooked until it forms a golden crust on the outside while remaining soft and creamy on the inside. Its origins can be traced back to the early 19th century in the Basque Country, and it has since become a symbol of Spanish cuisine.

Gazpacho
A refreshing cold soup, gazpacho is a quintessential Spanish dish, particularly popular during the hot summer months. Made from ripe tomatoes, cucumbers, bell peppers, onions, garlic, olive oil, and vinegar, gazpacho is blended to a smooth consistency and served chilled. It has its roots in the southern region of Andalusia, where the farmers would mix the fresh ingredients together to create a revitalizing meal during the scorching summers.

Churros
These deep-fried dough pastries are a beloved Spanish treat, often enjoyed for breakfast or as a snack. Made from a simple batter of flour, water, and salt, churros are piped through a star-shaped nozzle and fried until crispy. They are traditionally served with a cup of thick hot chocolate for dipping. Churros have a long history in Spain, with references to similar pastries dating back to the 16th century.

Patatas Bravas
A classic tapas dish, patatas bravas consists of crispy fried potatoes served with a spicy tomato sauce and creamy aioli. This dish has humble origins, originating as a hearty and affordable street food option in Madrid. Over time, it has become a staple in tapas bars and restaurants across Spain, loved for its contrasting textures and bold flavors.

Gambas al Ajillo

Gambas al Ajillo is a timeless Spanish tapas dish that embodies the essence of Mediterranean coastal cuisine. This exquisite dish features plump and succulent shrimp, lovingly cooked in a fragrant blend of garlic-infused olive oil, with a hint of chili for a touch of warmth. The aromatic herbs and zesty lemon juice add a burst of freshness, elevating the flavors to new heights. Gambas al Ajillo is a true celebration of the sea, where the delicate sweetness of the shrimp harmonizes with the robust and earthy notes of garlic, resulting in a symphony of flavors that dance on the palate.

With a history deeply rooted in the coastal regions of Spain, Gambas al Ajillo has been enjoyed for generations. The dish originated as a humble creation of fishermen, who would cook their fresh catch with simple and readily available ingredients. As the aroma of sizzling garlic and shrimp wafted through the air, it became a symbol of their love for the sea and their appreciation for the bountiful treasures it provided.

4 SERVINGS | 15 MINUTES | 200 KCAL | EASY

INGREDIENTS

- 1 pound large shrimp, peeled and deveined, with tails intact
- 4 cloves of garlic, thinly sliced
- 1 dried chili pepper, crushed (optional)
- 1/4 cup extra virgin olive oil
- 2 tablespoons fresh parsley, finely chopped
- 1 tablespoon lemon juice
- Salt and pepper to taste

GARLIC

Garlic is not only renowned for its rich and aromatic flavor but also for its impressive nutritional profile. Packed with vitamins, minerals, and antioxidants, garlic is known to support heart health, boost the immune system, reduce inflammation, and offer potential antimicrobial properties.

DIRECTIONS

1. In a large skillet or frying pan, heat the olive oil over medium heat.
2. Add the sliced garlic and crushed chili pepper to the pan. Sauté until the garlic turns golden and becomes fragrant, taking care not to burn it.
3. Increase the heat to medium-high and add the shrimp to the pan. Cook for about 2 minutes on each side until they turn pink and opaque. Be careful not to overcook the shrimp, as they can become rubbery.
4. Sprinkle the shrimp with salt, pepper, and fresh parsley. Toss gently to coat the shrimp evenly with the aromatic flavors.
5. Remove the pan from the heat and drizzle the lemon juice over the shrimp, giving them a final burst of freshness.
6. Transfer the Gambas al Ajillo to a serving dish, ensuring to pour the flavorful garlic-infused olive oil over the top.
7. Serve immediately as a tapas dish or as a main course, accompanied by crusty bread to soak up the delicious oil and juices

Notes:

1. Gambas al Ajillo is best enjoyed with fresh and high-quality shrimp, as they are the star of the dish. Look for firm, plump shrimp with a sweet aroma.
2. For added heat, you can increase the amount of chili pepper or add a pinch of red pepper flakes.
3. The lemon juice adds a refreshing touch to the dish, but feel free to adjust the amount to suit your taste preference.
4. Serve Gambas al Ajillo as part of a tapas spread or as a main course with a side of rice or crusty bread and a simple green salad.
5. This dish is perfect for entertaining guests or for a cozy night in, allowing you to savor the flavors of Spain in every delicious bite.

Enjoy the tantalizing flavors of Gambas al Ajillo, where succulent shrimp, fragrant garlic, and aromatic herbs unite to create a taste sensation that transports you to the sun-kissed shores of Spain.

Croquetas de Jamón

Croquetas de Jamón, the beloved Spanish ham croquettes, are a culinary delight that combines creamy béchamel sauce with the savory richness of cured ham, enveloped in a golden and crispy breadcrumb coating. With their origins deeply rooted in Spanish gastronomy, Croquetas de Jamón have become an integral part of the country's culinary heritage.

The history of Croquetas de Jamón can be traced back to the royal courts of Spain, where they were initially created as a luxurious indulgence enjoyed by the aristocracy. Over time, the popularity of these delectable croquettes spread across all social classes, and they became a common feature in Spanish cuisine. Today, they are a staple in tapas bars and home kitchens throughout the country.

To prepare these mouthwatering croquettes, finely chopped cooked ham is gently sautéed in butter, infusing the mixture with its distinctive flavor. A velvety béchamel sauce is then crafted by blending flour, milk, and spices, creating a luscious base that binds the ham together. This mixture is cooled, allowing it to solidify and develop its characteristic texture.

4 SERVINGS | 45 MINUTES | 150 KCAL | MED

INGREDIENTS

- 1 cup cooked ham, finely chopped
- 3 tablespoons unsalted butter
- 1/4 cup all-purpose flour
- 1 1/2 cups whole milk
- 1/4 teaspoon ground nutmeg
- Salt and pepper to taste
- 2 large eggs, beaten
- 1 cup fine breadcrumbs
- Vegetable oil, for frying

DIRECTIONS

1. In a medium-sized saucepan, melt the butter over medium heat. Add the chopped ham and sauté for 2-3 minutes until lightly browned and fragrant.
2. Sprinkle the flour over the ham and stir continuously for 1 minute, ensuring the ham is well-coated with the flour.
3. Gradually pour in the milk, whisking constantly to prevent lumps from forming. Cook the mixture for about 5 minutes until it thickens to a smooth and creamy consistency, resembling a béchamel sauce.
4. Stir in the ground nutmeg and season with salt and pepper to taste. Continue cooking for an additional 2-3 minutes, stirring continuously to ensure the flavors are well incorporated.
5. Remove the saucepan from the heat and transfer the mixture to a shallow dish. Allow it to cool completely, then cover and refrigerate for at least 2 hours or until firm.
6. Once the mixture has cooled and solidified, take about 1 tablespoon of the mixture and shape it into a small cylinder or oval shape using your hands. Repeat until all the mixture is used.
7. Dip each croquette into the beaten eggs, ensuring it is well coated, then roll it in the breadcrumbs until evenly coated. Place the coated croquettes on a baking sheet and refrigerate for 15-20 minutes to set.
8. In a large skillet or deep fryer, heat vegetable oil to approximately 350°F (175°C). Fry the croquettes in batches for 3-4 minutes until golden brown and crispy. Remove with a slotted spoon and drain on paper towels.
9. Serve the Croquetas de Jamón warm as a delightful tapas dish, accompanied by a tangy dipping sauce or a simple squeeze of lemon.

Notes:

1. The ham used in this recipe can be any cured or cooked ham, such as serrano ham or leftover holiday ham.
2. The key to achieving the perfect croquette texture is to allow the mixture to cool and firm up in the refrigerator before shaping and coating.
3. You can customize the shape and size of the croquettes to suit your preference, whether it be small bite-sized pieces or larger portions.

Albondigas

Albóndigas, the beloved Spanish meatballs, are a culinary delight that embodies the heart and soul of Spanish comfort food. These tender and juicy meatballs are a testament to the rich culinary history of Spain, with their origins dating back to the Moorish influence on the Iberian Peninsula. Albóndigas have since become an iconic dish, cherished for their exquisite blend of flavors and their ability to bring people together around the table.

The beauty of Albóndigas lies in the simplicity of its ingredients and the depth of its flavors. Ground beef, or a combination of beef and pork, is mixed with breadcrumbs, milk, onions, garlic, and a medley of aromatic herbs and spices. This flavorful mixture is carefully shaped into small, bite-sized meatballs, which are then lovingly cooked to perfection.

The tomato sauce that envelops the meatballs is a key component of Albóndigas, infusing them with a rich and tangy flavor. Sautéed onions and garlic provide a fragrant base, while crushed tomatoes, broth, and a blend of paprika and oregano create a vibrant and savory sauce. As the meatballs simmer gently in the sauce, they absorb its essence, becoming even more tender and flavorful.

4 SERVINGS | 30 MINUTES | 300 KCAL | MED

INGREDIENTS

For the meatballs:
- 1 pound ground beef (or a mix of beef and pork)
- 1/2 cup breadcrumbs
- 1/4 cup milk
- 1 small onion, finely chopped
- 2 cloves garlic, minced
- 1/4 cup fresh parsley, chopped
- 1 teaspoon ground cumin
- 1 teaspoon paprika
- 1/2 teaspoon dried oregano
- Salt and pepper to taste
- 1 large egg, beaten
- Olive oil, for frying

For the tomato sauce:
- 2 tablespoons olive oil
- 1 small onion, finely chopped
- 2 cloves garlic, minced
- 1 can (14 ounces) crushed tomatoes
- 1 cup chicken or vegetable broth
- 1 teaspoon paprika
- 1/2 teaspoon dried oregano
- Salt and pepper to taste
- Fresh parsley, for garnish

DIRECTIONS

1. In a large bowl, combine the ground beef, breadcrumbs, milk, onion, garlic, parsley, cumin, paprika, dried oregano, salt, and pepper. Mix well to ensure all the ingredients are evenly incorporated.
2. Add the beaten egg to the mixture and continue mixing until it forms a cohesive mixture. If the mixture feels too wet, add a little more breadcrumbs; if it feels too dry, add a splash of milk.
3. Shape the meat mixture into small meatballs, about 1 inch in diameter. Place them on a baking sheet lined with parchment paper.
4. Heat olive oil in a large skillet over medium heat. Add the meatballs in batches, ensuring they have enough space to brown evenly. Cook for about 3-4 minutes on each side until golden brown. Remove the cooked meatballs from the skillet and set them aside.
5. In the same skillet, add 2 tablespoons of olive oil and sauté the chopped onion until softened and translucent. Add the minced garlic and cook for an additional minute.
6. Stir in the crushed tomatoes, chicken or vegetable broth, paprika, dried oregano, salt, and pepper. Bring the sauce to a simmer and cook for about 10 minutes, allowing the flavors to meld together.
7. Return the cooked meatballs to the skillet, nestling them gently into the tomato sauce. Reduce the heat to low and let the meatballs simmer in the sauce for 15-20 minutes, allowing them to absorb the flavors.
8. Serve the Albóndigas hot, garnished with fresh parsley. They can be enjoyed as a tapas dish, served with crusty bread, or as a main course with rice or pasta.

Notes:
1. Albóndigas can be made with different types of meat, such as beef, pork, or a combination of both. Feel free to experiment and use your preferred meat blend.
2. The breadcrumbs and milk mixture helps keep the meatballs moist and tender. If you prefer a gluten-free version, you can use gluten-free breadcrumbs or substitute with almond flour.
3. These meatballs can be prepared in advance and refrigerated for a few hours or overnight to allow the flavors to develop further.

Pimientos de Padrón

Pimientos de Padrón, the iconic Spanish dish, transports you to the sun-drenched streets of Spain with its simplicity and explosive flavors. These small, green peppers, hailing from the town of Padrón in Galicia, are renowned for their delicate taste and tantalizing texture. With a history dating back centuries, Pimientos de Padrón have become an integral part of Spanish culinary culture and a beloved tapas favorite.

The beauty of Pimientos de Padrón lies in their unpredictability. While most of the peppers are mild and slightly sweet, there is always the chance of encountering a fiery surprise. This element of culinary Russian roulette adds excitement and anticipation to each bite, making them a delightful treat for adventurous palates.

To prepare Pimientos de Padrón, the peppers are simply sautéed in olive oil until they blister and char, creating a smoky and alluring aroma. The heat of the skillet transforms the peppers, bringing out their natural sweetness and adding a touch of charred richness. Once cooked, the peppers are generously sprinkled with sea salt, creating a harmonious balance between the mild sweetness of the pepper and the savory burst of salt.

4 SERVINGS | 10 MINUTES | 80 KCAL | EASY

INGREDIENTS

- 1 pound Padrón peppers
- 2 tablespoons olive oil
- Sea salt, to taste

DIRECTIONS

1. Rinse the Padrón peppers under cold water and pat them dry with a kitchen towel.
2. Heat the olive oil in a large skillet over medium-high heat.
3. Add the peppers to the skillet in a single layer, ensuring they have enough space to cook evenly.
4. Cook the peppers for 5-6 minutes, turning them occasionally, until the skins blister and char in spots.
5. Once the peppers are cooked, remove them from the skillet and transfer them to a serving plate lined with paper towels to drain any excess oil.
6. Sprinkle the peppers generously with sea salt while they are still hot. The salt will adhere to the peppers, enhancing their flavors.
7. Serve the Pimientos de Padrón immediately as a tapas dish or side accompaniment. Remember to inform your guests that the peppers can vary in heat, with some being mild and others carrying a surprising spiciness.
8. To enjoy, simply pick up a pepper by its stem, hold it by the tip, and bite into the tender flesh, savoring the smoky, salty, and slightly sweet taste.

Notes:

1. Padrón peppers are typically mild, but occasionally, you may come across a spicy one. This element of surprise adds to the excitement of eating Pimientos de Padrón.
2. The blistered skins of the peppers are part of their charm, adding a rustic and visually appealing element to the dish.
3. Pimientos de Padrón are traditionally served as a tapas dish, allowing people to share and savor their unique flavors together.
4. It is best to use a high-quality olive oil to enhance the taste of the peppers and add a touch of richness.
5. Enjoy the addictive allure of Pimientos de Padrón, where each bite brings a burst of flavor and a touch of Spanish culinary tradition. Whether enjoyed as a tapas dish, a snack, or a side dish, these peppers offer a delightful taste experience that embodies the vibrant and diverse flavors of Spanish cuisine.

Boquerones en Vinagre

Boquerones en Vinagre, a revered Spanish delicacy, celebrates the coastal bounty of Spain with its exquisite flavors and time-honored preparation. This tapas dish features fresh anchovies, or boquerones, that are transformed through a process of marinating in vinegar, infusing them with a delightful tang and enhancing their delicate brininess.

Originating from the coastal regions of Spain, where seafood reigns supreme, Boquerones en Vinagre has become a beloved part of Spanish culinary heritage. With a history that spans generations, this dish reflects the rich fishing traditions that have shaped the gastronomy of the country's coastal communities.

The preparation of Boquerones en Vinagre requires precision and care. Fresh anchovies are meticulously cleaned, removing the heads and guts while keeping the delicate fillets intact. The anchovies are then arranged in layers in a dish, interspersed with slices of garlic, sprinkles of fresh parsley, and a hint of red pepper flakes for those seeking a touch of heat.

4 SERVINGS   20 MINUTES   100 KCAL   MED

INGREDIENTS

- 1 pound fresh anchovies (boquerones)
- 1 cup white wine vinegar
- 4 cloves garlic, thinly sliced
- 1/4 cup fresh parsley, chopped
- 1/4 teaspoon red pepper flakes (optional)
- Extra virgin olive oil, for drizzling
- Sea salt, to taste

DIRECTIONS

1. Rinse the fresh anchovies under cold water and pat them dry with a paper towel.
2. Using a sharp knife, remove the heads and guts of the anchovies, gently pulling out the backbone to open them flat.
3. In a glass or ceramic dish, arrange a layer of anchovies, skin side down, in a single layer.
4. Sprinkle the anchovies with a layer of sliced garlic, a sprinkle of chopped parsley, and a pinch of red pepper flakes if desired.
5. Repeat the layering process, alternating anchovies and the remaining ingredients until all the anchovies are used.
6. Pour the white wine vinegar over the anchovies, ensuring they are completely submerged in the liquid.
7. Cover the dish with plastic wrap and refrigerate for at least 4 hours, or preferably overnight, allowing the flavors to meld and the anchovies to marinate.
8. After marinating, remove the anchovies from the dish and gently pat them dry with a paper towel, removing any excess liquid.
9. Transfer the anchovies to a serving plate, arranging them in a single layer.
10. Drizzle the anchovies with extra virgin olive oil and sprinkle with sea salt to taste.
11. Serve the Boquerones en Vinagre chilled, either as a standalone tapas dish or as part of a larger spread of Spanish delicacies.

Notes:

1. Boquerones en Vinagre can be enjoyed as a tapas dish, paired with crusty bread, olives, and other Spanish treats. They can also be used as a topping for salads, pizzas, or even enjoyed on their own as a light and flavorful appetizer.
2. The marinating process not only enhances the flavors of the anchovies but also helps to tenderize the flesh, making them wonderfully succulent.
3. Quality ingredients, such as fresh anchovies and a good white wine vinegar, are key to achieving the best flavor and texture.
4. Boquerones en Vinagre can be stored in the refrigerator for up to a week, allowing you to enjoy their deliciousness over several days.

ANCHOVIES

Anchovies are a nutritional powerhouse, packed with essential nutrients. They are an excellent source of protein, omega-3 fatty acids, calcium, and iron. These small fish are also rich in vitamins like vitamin A, vitamin D, and vitamin B12, making them a nutrient-dense addition to your diet.

Pulpo a la Gallega

Pulpo a la Gallega, a celebrated Spanish delicacy originating from the coastal region of Galicia, captures the essence of the sea in a tantalizing dish. This traditional recipe highlights the art of transforming octopus into a tender and flavorful masterpiece. With its rich history deeply rooted in Galician fishing traditions, Pulpo a la Gallega has become an emblematic dish that embodies the unique culinary heritage of the region.

The key to the exceptional taste of Pulpo a la Gallega lies in the careful preparation of the octopus. Once cleaned and rinsed, the octopus is simmered gently in a fragrant broth until it reaches the perfect tenderness. The long cooking process allows the octopus to release its natural flavors and transforms its flesh into a succulent and delicate texture.

Accompanying the star ingredient, thinly sliced potatoes create a luscious and hearty foundation for the dish. Boiled until tender, the potatoes absorb the subtle flavors of the cooking liquid, adding earthy sweetness and a delightful contrast to the tender octopus.

4 SERVINGS | 60 MINUTES | 300 KCAL | MED

INGREDIENTS

- 2 pounds octopus, cleaned and rinsed
- 4 large potatoes, peeled and sliced
- 1/4 cup extra virgin olive oil
- 2 tablespoons sweet paprika
- Sea salt, to taste
- Fresh parsley, chopped (for garnish)
- Lemon wedges (for serving)

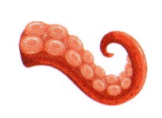

DIRECTIONS

1. Fill a large pot with water and bring it to a boil over high heat. Add a pinch of salt.
2. Carefully place the octopus in the pot, making sure it is fully submerged in the boiling water.
3. Reduce the heat to medium-low and simmer the octopus for approximately 45-60 minutes, or until it becomes tender. To check for doneness, insert a fork or knife into the thickest part of the octopus. It should easily slide in and out.
4. While the octopus is cooking, prepare the potatoes. Place the sliced potatoes in a separate pot, cover them with water, and add a pinch of salt. Bring to a boil and cook until the potatoes are tender. Drain and set aside.
5. Once the octopus is cooked, remove it from the pot and allow it to cool slightly. Cut it into thin slices, about 1/4 inch thick.
6. Arrange the sliced potatoes on a serving platter, creating a bed for the octopus.
7. Place the sliced octopus on top of the potatoes, drizzling it with extra virgin olive oil.
8. Sprinkle the dish with sweet paprika, ensuring it is evenly distributed over the octopus and potatoes.
9. Season with sea salt to taste and garnish with freshly chopped parsley.
10. Serve Pulpo a la Gallega warm, accompanied by lemon wedges for a touch of acidity. It is traditionally enjoyed as a tapas dish or as part of a larger Galician feast.

Notes:

1. To achieve a tender octopus, it is important to simmer it gently and avoid overcooking, as this can result in a rubbery texture.
2. Some recipes suggest adding a cork or a bay leaf to the cooking water to help tenderize the octopus, but this step is optional.
3. Pulpo a la Gallega is a dish that showcases the simplicity and quality of its ingredients. The focus is on allowing the natural flavors of the octopus and the earthy sweetness of the potatoes to shine.
4. This dish can be served as a tapas offering, or as a main course accompanied by a fresh green salad and crusty bread.

OCTOPUS

Octopus is a nutritional powerhouse, packed with essential nutrients. It is low in fat, high in protein, and rich in vitamins and minerals such as vitamin B12, iron, and potassium. Octopus is also a good source of omega-3 fatty acids, making it a healthy and delicious addition to your diet.

Pinchos de Pollo

Pinchos de Pollo, a delectable Spanish dish, captures the essence of Mediterranean flavors in bite-sized pieces. With its roots deeply embedded in Spanish culinary traditions, pinchos de pollo have evolved into a beloved tapas dish that brings people together. Tender chunks of chicken are marinated in a flavorful blend of olive oil, citrus juice, and aromatic spices, then skewered and grilled to perfection. The result is a succulent and juicy delight that showcases the art of simplicity and the boldness of Spanish cuisine.

Pinchos de Pollo have a rich history that can be traced back to the bustling streets of Spain, where food vendors and outdoor markets are filled with the aromas of sizzling skewers. These tantalizing treats are a popular choice at social gatherings, fiestas, and tapas bars, where friends and family gather to share in the joy of good food and lively conversation.

The marinade plays a crucial role in infusing the chicken with flavor and tenderness. A harmonious combination of olive oil, lemon juice, garlic, smoked paprika, cumin, oregano, salt, and pepper creates a vibrant medley of tastes that elevate the humble chicken to new heights. The marinade not only imparts a tangy and smoky essence but also helps to lock in moisture, resulting in juicy and succulent pieces of chicken.

4 SERVINGS **30 MINUTES** **200 KCAL** **EASY**

INGREDIENTS

- 1 pound boneless, skinless chicken breast, cut into bite-sized cubes
- 1/4 cup olive oil
- 2 tablespoons fresh lemon juice
- 2 cloves garlic, minced
- 1 teaspoon smoked paprika
- 1 teaspoon ground cumin
- 1/2 teaspoon dried oregano
- 1/2 teaspoon salt
- 1/4 teaspoon black pepper
- Wooden skewers, soaked in water for 30 minutes

DIRECTIONS

1. In a bowl, combine the olive oil, lemon juice, minced garlic, smoked paprika, ground cumin, dried oregano, salt, and black pepper. Whisk together until well blended.
2. Add the chicken cubes to the marinade and toss until evenly coated. Cover the bowl and refrigerate for at least 1 hour, allowing the flavors to infuse into the chicken.
3. Preheat the grill to medium-high heat.
4. Remove the chicken from the marinade and thread the pieces onto the soaked wooden skewers.
5. Place the skewers on the preheated grill and cook for about 8-10 minutes, turning occasionally, until the chicken is cooked through and slightly charred on the outside.
6. Transfer the cooked pinchos de pollo to a serving platter and let them rest for a few minutes before serving.
7. Serve the pinchos de pollo hot as a standalone tapas dish or as part of a larger Spanish spread. They pair perfectly with a variety of dipping sauces, such as aioli, salsa verde, or romesco sauce.
8. Enjoy the flavorful and succulent pinchos de pollo with friends and family, savoring each bite as you immerse yourself in the vibrant and enticing world of Spanish cuisine.

Notes:

1. For a variation, you can add chunks of bell peppers, onions, or cherry tomatoes between the chicken cubes on the skewers to add color and additional flavors.
2. If you don't have a grill, you can also cook the pinchos de pollo on a stovetop grill pan or even in the oven under the broiler.
3. Pinchos de pollo are versatile and can be served as an appetizer, a main course, or even in sandwiches or wraps.
4. Embrace the spirit of Spanish cuisine with pinchos de pollo, where the combination of smoky spices and succulent chicken brings a burst of flavor to your palate.

Pan con Tomate

Pan con Tomate, a beloved Spanish dish, captures the essence of Mediterranean simplicity and freshness. This traditional recipe is a delightful celebration of two staple ingredients: crusty bread and ripe tomatoes. Originating from the regions of Catalonia and Valencia, Pan con Tomate has deep roots in Spanish culinary traditions and has become a culinary icon that embodies the vibrant and flavorful essence of the Mediterranean diet.

The history of Pan con Tomate dates back centuries, when Spanish families found a creative way to repurpose stale bread. By rubbing ripe tomatoes onto the bread, they transformed it into a delicious and refreshing treat. Over time, this humble dish gained popularity and became a cherished part of Spanish cuisine.

To make Pan con Tomate, start by selecting a large, ripe tomato. Cut it in half and rub the cut side of the tomato onto each slice of bread, allowing the sweet and tangy juices to permeate the crust. This simple act infuses the bread with the vibrant flavors of ripe tomatoes, creating a refreshing and aromatic base.

4 SERVINGS | **15 MINUTES** | **200 KCAL** | **EASY**

INGREDIENTS

- 1 large ripe tomato
- 4 slices of rustic bread, preferably crusty
- 2 cloves of garlic, peeled
- Extra virgin olive oil
- Sea salt, to taste

DIRECTIONS

1. Preheat a grill pan or toaster.
2. Cut the tomato in half and rub the cut side of the tomato onto each slice of bread, ensuring that the bread is evenly coated with the tomato juices. This will impart a fresh and tangy flavor to the bread.
3. Once the bread is coated with tomato, lightly toast the slices on the grill pan or in the toaster until they are golden brown and slightly crispy.
4. While the bread is still warm, take a garlic clove and rub it over each slice, allowing the garlic to infuse its aroma into the bread. The amount of garlic can be adjusted according to personal preference.
5. Drizzle each slice of bread with a generous amount of extra virgin olive oil, ensuring that it soaks into the bread.
6. Sprinkle a pinch of sea salt over each slice to enhance the flavors and add a hint of savory goodness.
7. Serve Pan con Tomate immediately, while the bread is still warm and crisp. It can be enjoyed as a simple snack, as an accompaniment to charcuterie or cheese, or as a side dish to a Spanish meal.
8. Experience the delightful simplicity of Pan con Tomate, where the juicy sweetness of ripe tomatoes, the crunch of crusty bread, and the richness of olive oil come together to create a taste sensation that transports you to the sun-drenched landscapes of Spain.

Notes:

1. For an extra burst of flavor, you can experiment with additional toppings such as sliced serrano ham, grated Manchego cheese, or fresh basil leaves.
2. Choose high-quality ingredients, as they are essential to achieving the authentic and vibrant flavors of Pan con Tomate.
3. This dish is best enjoyed during the tomato season when ripe and juicy tomatoes are abundant.
4. Pan con Tomate is a versatile dish that can be adapted to personal preferences. Some variations include adding a sprinkle of paprika or a drizzle of balsamic reduction for added depth of flavor.
5. Embrace the art of simplicity and the essence of Spanish cuisine with Pan con Tomate, where a few basic ingredients combine to create a satisfying and delicious dish that celebrates the flavors of the Mediterranean.

Ensaladilla Rusa

Ensaladilla Rusa, also known as Russian Salad, is a classic Spanish dish that has become an integral part of the country's culinary culture. This delightful salad is a harmonious medley of cooked vegetables, eggs, and mayonnaise, creating a creamy and flavorful dish that is loved by all. Despite its name, Ensaladilla Rusa has deep Spanish roots and has been adapted to suit the local palate. It has become a staple in Spanish households, particularly during celebrations, gatherings, and picnics.

Originating in Russia during the 19th century, the original Russian Salad consisted of cooked vegetables, meat, and mayonnaise. The recipe traveled across Europe and found its way to Spain, where it was embraced and modified to incorporate local ingredients and flavors. Over time, the Spanish version of the salad, Ensaladilla Rusa, evolved into its own unique dish.

Ensaladilla Rusa is a versatile and customizable recipe that can vary from region to region and from household to household. The essential ingredients include cooked potatoes, carrots, peas, and boiled eggs, mixed with mayonnaise. Additional ingredients such as tuna, olives, pickles, or cooked ham can be added according to personal preference.

4 SERVINGS | 30 MINUTES | 300 KCAL | EASY

INGREDIENTS

- 2 medium potatoes, boiled and diced
- 2 carrots, boiled and diced
- 1 cup green peas, boiled
- 4 boiled eggs, chopped
- 1/2 cup mayonnaise
- 1 can tuna (optional)
- Salt and pepper, to taste
- Olives and pickles, for garnish (optional)

DIRECTIONS

1. In a large bowl, combine the diced potatoes, carrots, peas, and chopped eggs.
2. Add mayonnaise to the bowl and gently mix until all the ingredients are well coated. Adjust the amount of mayonnaise according to desired creaminess.
3. If using, drain the canned tuna and add it to the salad. Gently fold it in to incorporate.
4. Season the salad with salt and pepper to taste. Be mindful of the saltiness of the canned tuna, if using.
5. Once all the ingredients are well combined, cover the bowl and refrigerate for at least 1 hour to allow the flavors to meld together.
6. Before serving, give the Ensaladilla Rusa a final stir and adjust the seasoning if needed.
7. Garnish with olives and pickles, if desired, for an extra burst of flavor and visual appeal.
8. Serve the Ensaladilla Rusa chilled as a refreshing tapas dish or as a side to grilled meats or fish.
9. Enjoy the creamy and satisfying Ensaladilla Rusa, savoring the blend of textures and flavors that make it a beloved classic in Spanish cuisine.

Notes:

1. Ensaladilla Rusa can be prepared in advance and stored in the refrigerator for up to 2 days, making it a convenient option for gatherings and parties.
2. Experiment with additional ingredients such as diced cooked ham, roasted red peppers, or capers to personalize the salad according to your taste preferences.
3. This versatile salad can be adapted to suit dietary preferences by using vegan mayonnaise or substituting ingredients to accommodate specific dietary needs.
4. Experience the charm of Ensaladilla Rusa, a culinary treasure that has stood the test of time and continues to bring joy to Spanish tables.

Mejillones en Escabeche

Mejillones en Escabeche is a delightful Spanish dish that showcases the vibrant flavors of the sea. It consists of fresh mussels cooked in a tangy and aromatic marinade, resulting in a tantalizing combination of textures and tastes. With its roots in Spain's rich culinary heritage, Mejillones en Escabeche has become a beloved tapas dish, adored for its robust flavors and versatility.

The history of Mejillones en Escabeche can be traced back to the traditional preservation techniques used in Spain to extend the shelf life of seafood. Escabeche, a method of pickling or marinating food in vinegar, was employed as a way to preserve mussels and other seafood in the days before refrigeration. The acidic marinade not only added flavor but also acted as a natural preservative, allowing people to enjoy the flavors of the sea even when fresh seafood was not readily available.

Today, Mejillones en Escabeche has evolved into a popular tapas dish that showcases the culinary ingenuity of Spain. Fresh mussels are steamed until they open, revealing their plump and succulent meat. The cooked mussels are then marinated in a mixture of vinegar, olive oil, garlic, herbs, and spices, infusing them with a tantalizing blend of flavors.

4 SERVINGS   **30** MINUTES   **200** KCAL   **EASY**

INGREDIENTS

- 2 pounds fresh mussels, cleaned and debearded
- 1/2 cup white wine
- 1/2 cup white vinegar
- 1/4 cup extra virgin olive oil
- 4 cloves garlic, minced
- 1 teaspoon sweet paprika
- 1 bay leaf
- Salt and pepper, to taste
- Fresh parsley, for garnish

MUSSELS

Mussels are highly nutritious, offering a wealth of health benefits. They are an excellent source of lean protein, rich in vitamins and minerals such as vitamin B12, iron, selenium, and zinc. Additionally, mussels provide omega-3 fatty acids, which are beneficial for heart health and brain function.

DIRECTIONS

1. In a large pot, heat the white wine over medium-high heat until it simmers.
2. Add the mussels to the pot and cover with a lid. Steam the mussels for about 5 minutes or until they open.
3. Remove the mussels from the pot, discarding any that did not open. Set aside to cool.
4. In a separate saucepan, combine the white vinegar, olive oil, minced garlic, sweet paprika, bay leaf, salt, and pepper. Bring the mixture to a simmer and let it cook for a few minutes to infuse the flavors.
5. Remove the marinade from the heat and let it cool slightly.
6. Once the mussels have cooled, carefully remove the shells, leaving the meat intact.
7. Place the shelled mussels in a shallow dish or container and pour the marinade over them, ensuring they are fully submerged.
8. Cover the dish and refrigerate for at least 2 hours, allowing the flavors to meld together.
9. Before serving, garnish the Mejillones en Escabeche with fresh parsley for a pop of color and added freshness.
10. Serve the marinated mussels chilled as a tapas dish, accompanied by crusty bread or as part of a seafood platter.
11. Enjoy the exquisite flavors of Mejillones en Escabeche, savoring the delicate balance of tanginess, richness, and brininess that make it a cherished Spanish delicacy.

Notes:

1. Ensure that all the mussels are tightly closed before cooking. Discard any mussels that remain closed after cooking, as they may be unfit for consumption.
2. The marinade can be adjusted according to personal taste preferences. Add more vinegar for a tangier flavor or increase the amount of olive oil for richness.
3. Mejillones en Escabeche can be stored in the refrigerator for up to 3 days, allowing the flavors to intensify over time.
4. Embrace the culinary heritage of Spain with Mejillones en Escabeche, a delicious and versatile dish that pays homage to the country's passion for seafood and marinated flavors.

Chorizo al Vino

Chorizo al Vino is a classic Spanish dish that showcases the rich flavors of chorizo sausage and the depth of Spanish wine. This delightful recipe combines the smoky and savory qualities of chorizo with the robust and earthy notes of red wine, resulting in a dish that is bursting with flavor. Chorizo al Vino is a beloved tapas dish that has its roots in the culinary traditions of Spain. The history of Chorizo al Vino can be traced back to the vibrant culinary heritage of Spain, where both chorizo sausage and wine play integral roles in the gastronomy. Chorizo, a type of cured pork sausage seasoned with paprika and other spices, has been a staple ingredient in Spanish cuisine for centuries. It is prized for its intense flavor and versatility.

To create Chorizo al Vino, the chorizo sausage is first cooked to release its delicious oils and flavors. It is then simmered in a rich red wine sauce, allowing the flavors to meld together and infuse the sausage with the depth and complexity of the wine. The result is a tender and succulent chorizo that is soaked in a luscious wine-infused sauce.

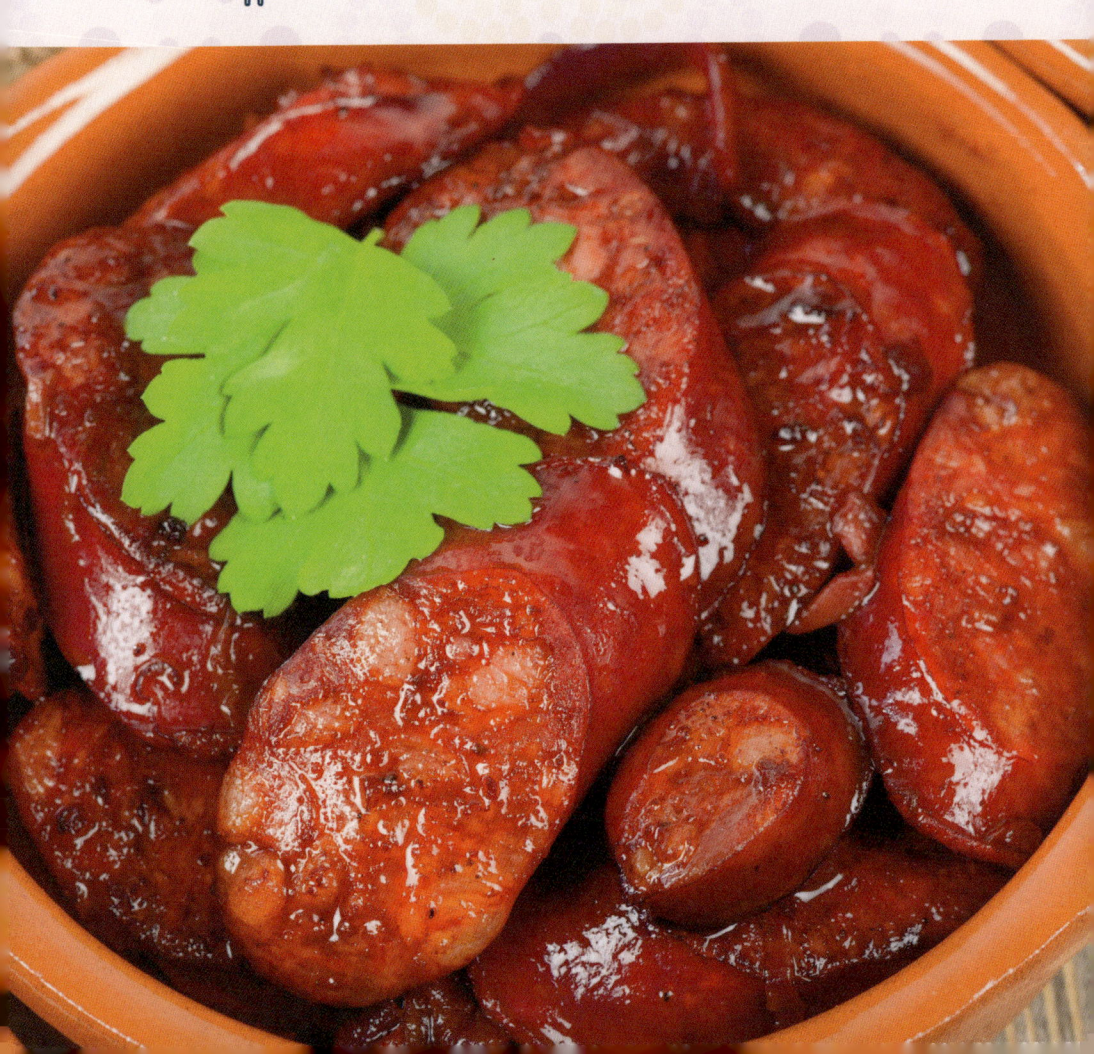

4 SERVINGS | **15 MINUTES** | **250 KCAL** | **EASY**

INGREDIENTS

- 1 pound chorizo sausage, sliced into bite-sized pieces
- 1 cup red wine (such as Rioja or Tempranillo)
- 2 cloves garlic, minced
- 1 tablespoon olive oil
- 1 teaspoon smoked paprika
- Fresh parsley, for garnish
- Crusty bread, for serving

DIRECTIONS

1. In a large skillet, heat the olive oil over medium heat. Add the chorizo slices and cook until they are browned and crispy on the outside, about 5 minutes.
2. Add the minced garlic and smoked paprika to the skillet, stirring to coat the chorizo in the aromatic flavors.
3. Pour in the red wine, stirring to combine. Bring the mixture to a simmer and let it cook for about 10 minutes, allowing the chorizo to absorb the flavors of the wine.
4. Reduce the heat to low and continue to simmer for another 10 minutes, allowing the wine sauce to thicken slightly.
5. Once the chorizo is cooked through and tender, remove the skillet from the heat.
6. Transfer the Chorizo al Vino to a serving dish and garnish with fresh parsley for added freshness and visual appeal.
7. Serve the dish warm with crusty bread on the side to soak up the flavorful wine sauce.
8. Enjoy the smoky and savory delight of Chorizo al Vino, savoring each bite as you immerse yourself in the rich culinary heritage of Spain.

Notes:

1. Experiment with different types of chorizo, such as spicy or mild, to suit your taste preferences.
2. Use a good-quality red wine that you enjoy drinking, as it will greatly enhance the flavor of the dish.
3. Leftovers of Chorizo al Vino can be refrigerated and enjoyed the next day, allowing the flavors to further develop and intensify.
4. Discover the essence of Spanish gastronomy with Chorizo al Vino, a delicious and satisfying dish that brings together the bold flavors of chorizo and the richness of red wine.

Calamares a la Romana

Calamares a la Romana is a beloved Spanish dish that showcases tender rings of calamari coated in a light and crispy batter. This delightful recipe is a popular choice for tapas, appetizers, or even as a main course. Calamares a la Romana is a testament to the rich culinary heritage of Spain and its love for seafood.

The history of Calamares a la Romana dates back to ancient Roman times when the Romans introduced the technique of frying food. Over the centuries, this dish has evolved and become a staple in Spanish cuisine. It is commonly found in coastal regions of Spain, where fresh seafood is abundant.

To prepare Calamares a la Romana, fresh calamari rings are coated in a simple batter made from flour, salt, and water. The calamari is then quickly deep-fried until golden and crispy, resulting in a delectable texture that contrasts beautifully with the tender interior. The dish is traditionally served with a squeeze of lemon juice, which adds a refreshing and tangy element to the fried calamari.

4 SERVINGS | 30 MINUTES | 250 KCAL | MED

INGREDIENTS

- 1 pound fresh calamari rings
- 1 cup all-purpose flour
- 1 teaspoon salt
- Vegetable oil, for frying
- Lemon wedges, for serving

DIRECTIONS

1. In a large mixing bowl, combine the flour and salt. Gradually add water, whisking until a smooth batter forms. The batter should have a consistency similar to pancake batter.
2. Heat vegetable oil in a deep fryer or large, deep skillet to a temperature of 350°F (175°C).
3. Dip the calamari rings into the batter, ensuring they are evenly coated. Shake off any excess batter.
4. Carefully lower the battered calamari rings into the hot oil, frying them in batches to avoid overcrowding the pan. Cook for approximately 2-3 minutes or until golden brown and crispy.
5. Using a slotted spoon or tongs, transfer the fried calamari rings to a plate lined with paper towels to drain excess oil.
6. Repeat the frying process with the remaining calamari rings until all are cooked.
7. Once the Calamares a la Romana are ready, transfer them to a serving platter.
8. Serve the Calamares a la Romana hot with lemon wedges on the side for squeezing over the crispy rings.
9. Enjoy the irresistible combination of tender calamari encased in a light and crispy batter, savoring the flavors and textures that make Calamares a la Romana a true Spanish delicacy.

Notes:

1. It is important to ensure that the oil is at the correct temperature before frying the calamari to achieve optimal crispiness.
2. Serve the Calamares a la Romana immediately to maintain their crispy texture.
3. Experiment with different dipping sauces such as aioli, tartar sauce, or spicy tomato-based sauces to complement the flavors of the fried calamari.
4. Embrace the culinary traditions of Spain with Calamares a la Romana, a delicious and satisfying dish that highlights the country's love for seafood and the art of frying.

PERFECT FRIED!

To achieve perfectly fried food, ensure that the oil is at the correct temperature before frying. Use a deep-fry thermometer to monitor the temperature and maintain it around 350-375°F (175-190°C). This will result in a crispy exterior while ensuring the interior cooks evenly and remains tender.

Berenjenas Fritas

Berenjenas Fritas is a classic Spanish dish that showcases the versatility of eggplant in a simple yet flavorful way. This delightful recipe features tender slices of eggplant that are lightly battered and fried to perfection, resulting in a crispy and delicious dish. Berenjenas Fritas is a popular tapas dish in Spain, loved for its addictive texture and delightful combination of flavors.

The history of Berenjenas Fritas can be traced back to the rich culinary traditions of Spain, where eggplants have been cultivated and used in various dishes for centuries. Eggplant is believed to have originated in the Indian subcontinent and was introduced to Spain during the Moorish rule. Since then, it has become an integral part of Spanish cuisine, and Berenjenas Fritas is just one of the many delicious ways it is prepared.

To prepare Berenjenas Fritas, the eggplant is sliced into thin rounds, salted, and left to sit for a while to draw out any bitterness. The excess moisture is then squeezed out, and the eggplant slices are coated in a light batter made from flour, salt, and water. The battered slices are deep-fried until golden brown and crispy, creating a satisfying contrast between the soft interior and crispy exterior.

4 SERVINGS | **30 MINUTES** | **200 KCAL** | **EASY**

INGREDIENTS

- 2 medium-sized eggplants
- Salt, for salting the eggplant
- 1 cup all-purpose flour
- 1 teaspoon salt
- Vegetable oil, for frying

DIRECTIONS

1. Slice the eggplants into thin rounds, approximately 1/4 inch thick.
2. Sprinkle salt over the eggplant slices and let them sit for about 30 minutes to draw out excess moisture and bitterness. Rinse the slices and pat them dry with a paper towel.
3. In a shallow dish, combine the flour and salt. Dredge each eggplant slice in the flour mixture, shaking off any excess.
4. Heat vegetable oil in a deep fryer or large, deep skillet to a temperature of 350°F (175°C).
5. Carefully place the battered eggplant slices into the hot oil, frying them in batches to avoid overcrowding the pan. Cook for approximately 3-4 minutes or until golden brown and crispy.
6. Use a slotted spoon or tongs to transfer the fried eggplant slices to a plate lined with paper towels to drain excess oil.
7. Repeat the frying process with the remaining eggplant slices until all are cooked.
8. Once the Berenjenas Fritas are ready, transfer them to a serving platter.
9. Serve the Berenjenas Fritas hot with a dipping sauce of your choice, such as aioli or romesco sauce.
10. Enjoy the crispy and flavorful delight of Berenjenas Fritas, savoring each bite as you immerse yourself in the rich culinary heritage of Spain.

Notes:

1. Ensure the oil is at the correct temperature before frying the eggplant slices to achieve optimal crispiness.
2. Adjust the seasoning of the flour mixture according to your taste preferences by adding herbs or spices.
3. Leftover Berenjenas Fritas can be reheated in the oven for a few minutes to regain their crispiness.
4. Experience the versatility of eggplant with Berenjenas Fritas, a delicious and satisfying dish that captures the essence of Spanish cuisine.

Queso Manchego

Queso Manchego is a renowned Spanish cheese that originates from the La Mancha region of Spain. This exquisite cheese is made from the milk of Manchega sheep and is celebrated for its distinctive flavor and creamy texture. Queso Manchego is a true testament to the rich cheese-making traditions of Spain and is beloved by cheese enthusiasts worldwide.

The history of Queso Manchego dates back centuries, with records of sheep farming and cheese production in the La Mancha region as early as the 12th century. The cheese gained protected designation of origin (PDO) status in 1984, ensuring that only cheese made from the milk of Manchega sheep in the La Mancha region can bear the name Queso Manchego.

To create Queso Manchego, the milk from Manchega sheep is carefully curdled and pressed. The cheese is then aged for a minimum of 60 days, although some varieties can be aged for up to two years. The aging process gives Queso Manchego its characteristic nutty and slightly tangy flavor, along with a firm yet buttery texture.

4 SERVINGS | - MINUTES | 100 KCAL | EASY

INGREDIENTS

- Manchega sheep's milk
- Salt
- Rennet (for coagulation)
- Cheese mold (for shaping)

DIRECTIONS

1. Heat the milk to a specific temperature and add rennet to coagulate the milk.
2. Cut the curds into small pieces and allow them to rest.
3. Drain the whey and transfer the curds into a cheese mold.
4. Apply pressure to the curds to shape the cheese.
5. Remove the cheese from the mold and immerse it in a brine solution for flavor development.
6. Age the cheese in a controlled environment, turning and monitoring it regularly.
7. Allow the cheese to age for a minimum of 60 days, or longer for a more intense flavor.
8. Once the desired aging period is reached, the Queso Manchego is ready to be enjoyed.
9. Serve the Queso Manchego at room temperature, allowing its flavors and textures to fully develop.
10. Pair the cheese with your favorite accompaniments, such as crusty bread, honey, or quince paste.
11. Appreciate the distinctive flavors and craftsmanship of Queso Manchego, savoring each bite as you indulge in this quintessential Spanish cheese.

Notes:

1. Queso Manchego is available in different aging categories, ranging from joven (young) to curado (aged), each offering unique characteristics.
2. Opt for Queso Manchego labeled with the PDO symbol to ensure authenticity and quality.
3. Experiment with different aging periods to discover your preferred flavor profile.
4. Experience the heritage and tradition of Spanish cheese-making with Queso Manchego, a true gastronomic treasure.

PERFECT FRIED!

To achieve perfectly fried food, ensure that the oil is at the correct temperature before frying. Use a deep-fry thermometer to monitor the temperature and maintain it around 350-375°F (175-190°C). This will result in a crispy exterior while ensuring the interior cooks evenly and remains tender.

Gazpacho

Gazpacho is a refreshing and vibrant Spanish cold soup that is perfect for hot summer days. This traditional dish originated in the southern region of Andalusia and has become a beloved staple of Spanish cuisine. Gazpacho showcases the essence of Mediterranean flavors with its combination of ripe tomatoes, crisp vegetables, and aromatic herbs.

The history of Gazpacho can be traced back to ancient times when Roman soldiers traveling through Spain carried a simple blend of bread, olive oil, and vinegar to create a basic soup. Over the centuries, the recipe evolved and incorporated local ingredients, eventually leading to the creation of Gazpacho as we know it today.

Gazpacho is characterized by its base of fresh tomatoes, cucumbers, bell peppers, onions, garlic, and bread. These ingredients are blended together with olive oil, vinegar, and a touch of salt to create a smooth and velvety texture. The soup is traditionally served chilled and garnished with diced vegetables, croutons, or a drizzle of olive oil.

The beauty of Gazpacho lies in its simplicity and versatility. It can be enjoyed as a light appetizer, a refreshing side dish, or even as a main course when paired with crusty bread.

4 SERVINGS | 20 MINUTES | 100 KCAL | EASY

INGREDIENTS

- 4 large ripe tomatoes, cored and chopped
- 1 cucumber, peeled, seeded, and chopped
- 1 red bell pepper, seeded and chopped
- 1 small red onion, chopped
- 2 cloves of garlic, minced
- 2 slices of stale bread, crust removed
- 1/4 cup extra-virgin olive oil
- 2 tablespoons red wine vinegar
- Salt, to taste
- Freshly ground black pepper, to taste
- Optional garnishes: diced cucumber, bell pepper, red onion, croutons, and a drizzle of olive oil

TOMATO POWER

Tomato soup is not only delicious but also packed with nutrients. Tomatoes are rich in vitamins A, C, and K, as well as antioxidants like lycopene, which has been linked to various health benefits. It is also low in calories and a good source of fiber.

DIRECTIONS

1. Place the chopped tomatoes, cucumber, red bell pepper, red onion, garlic, and stale bread in a blender or food processor.
2. Blend the ingredients until smooth and well combined.
3. While the blender is running, gradually add the olive oil and red wine vinegar, blending until incorporated.
4. Season the Gazpacho with salt and freshly ground black pepper, adjusting to taste.
5. Transfer the Gazpacho to a large bowl and refrigerate for at least 1 hour to chill and allow the flavors to meld.
6. Before serving, give the Gazpacho a good stir and adjust the seasoning if needed.
7. Ladle the chilled Gazpacho into individual bowls or glasses.
8. Garnish with diced cucumber, bell pepper, red onion, croutons, and a drizzle of olive oil, if desired.
9. Serve the Gazpacho chilled and enjoy its vibrant flavors and refreshing qualities.
10. Savor each spoonful of this traditional Spanish soup, appreciating the delicious blend of fresh ingredients that capture the essence of Mediterranean cuisine.

Notes:

1. Gazpacho is a versatile recipe that can be customized to personal taste preferences. Adjust the seasoning, acidity, or thickness according to your liking.
2. Feel free to experiment with additional ingredients such as fresh herbs, chili peppers, or even a splash of citrus juice to add a unique twist to your Gazpacho.
3. Gazpacho tastes best when made with ripe and flavorful tomatoes, so choose the best quality tomatoes available.
4. Embrace the flavors of Andalusia with Gazpacho, a refreshing and vibrant dish that represents the essence of Spanish cuisine.

Salmorejo

Salmorejo is a traditional Spanish cold soup that originates from the Andalusian region, specifically Cordoba. This delightful dish is a close relative of Gazpacho but offers its own unique flavors and texture. Salmorejo is known for its velvety consistency, vibrant color, and refreshing taste, making it a popular choice during the hot summer months.

Salmorejo has a fascinating history rooted in the culinary traditions of Andalusia. It is believed to have originated from Moorish influences, as the Moors introduced ingredients such as bread, vinegar, and olive oil to the Iberian Peninsula. Over time, these ingredients were combined with local produce like ripe tomatoes and garlic, resulting in the creation of Salmorejo.

The star ingredient of Salmorejo is ripe tomatoes, which provide the soup with its rich red color and sweet flavor. The tomatoes are blended together with bread, garlic, extra-virgin olive oil, and a splash of vinegar to create a smooth and creamy consistency. The addition of these ingredients gives Salmorejo a luxurious texture that distinguishes it from other cold soups.

Salmorejo is typically served chilled and garnished with diced hard-boiled eggs and jamón serrano or Spanish ham.

4 SERVINGS | 20 MINUTES | 150 KCAL | EASY

INGREDIENTS

- 1 kg ripe tomatoes, cored and roughly chopped
- 200 grams stale bread, crust removed and torn into pieces
- 2 cloves of garlic, minced
- 1/4 cup extra-virgin olive oil
- 1 tablespoon sherry vinegar or red wine vinegar
- Salt, to taste
- Optional garnishes: diced hard-boiled eggs, diced jamón serrano or Spanish ham, and a drizzle of olive oil

DIRECTIONS

1. Place the chopped tomatoes, bread, minced garlic, extra-virgin olive oil, and vinegar in a blender or food processor.
2. Blend the ingredients until smooth and well combined.
3. Season the mixture with salt, adjusting to taste.
4. Transfer the Salmorejo to a large bowl and refrigerate for at least 1 hour to chill and allow the flavors to meld.
5. Before serving, give the Salmorejo a good stir and adjust the seasoning if needed.
6. Ladle the chilled Salmorejo into individual bowls or glasses.
7. Garnish with diced hard-boiled eggs, diced jamón serrano or Spanish ham, and a drizzle of olive oil, if desired.
8. Serve the Salmorejo chilled and enjoy its velvety texture and refreshing flavors.
9. Accompany the soup with crusty bread for dipping, savoring the delightful combination of flavors.
10. Embrace the taste of Andalusia with Salmorejo, a traditional Spanish soup that showcases the beauty of ripe tomatoes and Mediterranean ingredients.

Notes:

1. The quality of the ingredients is crucial for a delicious Salmorejo. Choose ripe and flavorful tomatoes and use good-quality extra-virgin olive oil for the best results.
2. Adjust the consistency of the soup by adding more bread for a thicker texture or a splash of water for a lighter consistency.
3. Salmorejo can be stored in the refrigerator for a day or two, allowing the flavors to develop further.
4. Indulge in the cool and creamy delight of Salmorejo, experiencing the taste of Andalusia in every spoonful.

Caracoles a la Andaluza

Caracoles a la Andaluza, or Andalusian-style snails, is a traditional Spanish dish that showcases the flavors of the Andalusia region. This hearty and aromatic recipe features tender snails cooked in a flavorful broth with a combination of herbs, spices, and vegetables. Caracoles a la Andaluza is a beloved dish during festive occasions and is often enjoyed with a glass of sherry or local wine. The history of Caracoles a la Andaluza traces back to the culinary traditions of Andalusia, where snails have been consumed for centuries. Snails were abundant in the region and were gathered and prepared by locals as a delicious and nourishing food source. Over time, the recipe for Caracoles a la Andaluza evolved, incorporating local ingredients and culinary techniques to enhance the flavors and create a dish that has become an integral part of the regional cuisine. Caracoles a la Andaluza is a dish that requires time and patience to prepare, as the snails need to be cleaned thoroughly and cooked slowly to achieve the desired tenderness. The snails are typically simmered in a flavorful broth infused with garlic, onions, tomatoes, herbs like thyme and bay leaves, and spices such as paprika and cayenne pepper. This combination of ingredients creates a robust and aromatic base for the dish.

4 SERVINGS | 2 HOURS | 250 KCAL | MED

INGREDIENTS

- 1 kg fresh snails, cleaned and prepared
- 2 onions, finely chopped
- 4 cloves of garlic, minced
- 2 ripe tomatoes, peeled and diced
- 1 red bell pepper, diced
- 1 tablespoon sweet paprika
- 1/2 teaspoon cayenne pepper (optional, for added spice)
- 2 bay leaves
- 4 sprigs of thyme
- Salt, to taste
- Olive oil, for sautéing
- Water or broth, as needed

TOMATO POWER

Snails are not only a delicacy but also a nutritious ingredient. They are a good source of protein, low in fat, and rich in essential minerals like iron, magnesium, and calcium. Snails are also a good source of vitamins, including vitamin E and vitamin B12.

DIRECTIONS

1. Place the cleaned snails in a large pot and cover them with water. Bring to a boil and simmer for 10 minutes. Drain the snails and rinse them under cold water to remove any impurities.
2. In a separate large pot, heat olive oil over medium heat. Add the chopped onions and minced garlic, and sauté until softened and translucent.
3. Add the diced tomatoes and red bell pepper to the pot, and cook until they start to soften.
4. Stir in the sweet paprika and cayenne pepper, if using, and cook for a minute to release their flavors.
5. Add the drained snails to the pot, along with the bay leaves, thyme sprigs, and a pinch of salt. Stir well to coat the snails with the flavors of the ingredients.
6. Pour enough water or broth into the pot to cover the snails. Bring to a simmer and cook gently, partially covered, for about 1.5 to 2 hours, or until the snails are tender.
7. Taste the broth and adjust the seasoning with salt if needed.
8. Serve Caracoles a la Andaluza in individual bowls, along with some of the flavorful broth. It is customary to provide small forks or toothpicks to easily extract the snails from their shells.
9. Enjoy this delightful Andalusian dish with a glass of sherry or your favorite Spanish wine, savoring the rich flavors and the cultural heritage it represents.

Notes:

1. It is important to source fresh and high-quality snails for this recipe. If you are unable to find fresh snails, you can use pre-cooked or canned snails as a substitute.
2. The cooking time may vary depending on the size and tenderness of the snails. Adjust the cooking time accordingly to achieve the desired texture.
3. Caracoles a la Andaluza is often served as part of a tapas spread or enjoyed as a main course with crusty bread.
4. Embrace the flavors of Andalusia with Caracoles a la Andaluza, a traditional Spanish dish that celebrates the abundance of local ingredients and the culinary heritage of the region.

Tortillitas de Camarones

Tortillitas de Camarones, also known as Shrimp Fritters, is a traditional and beloved dish from the Andalusian region of Spain. These crispy and flavorful fritters are made with a batter of chickpea flour and shrimp, creating a delightful combination of textures and tastes. Tortillitas de Camarones is often enjoyed as a tapa or appetizer, showcasing the coastal influence of the Andalusian cuisine.

The history of Tortillitas de Camarones dates back to the fishing communities along the coast of Cadiz and Huelva, where shrimp was plentiful. The dish emerged as a creative way to incorporate shrimp into a simple and delicious recipe. It was traditionally prepared by local fishermen's wives who used the readily available ingredients and their culinary skills to craft these delightful fritters. Tortillitas de Camarones has become an iconic dish of the region, celebrated for its unique flavor and crunchy texture. It captures the essence of Andalusian cuisine, combining the freshness of the sea with the heartiness of chickpea flour. The fritters are often enjoyed with a squeeze of lemon juice, which adds a tangy and refreshing element to the dish.

4 SERVINGS | 30 MINUTES | 200 KCAL | EASY

INGREDIENTS

- 200 grams chickpea flour
- 200 grams small shrimp, peeled and deveined
- 1 small onion, finely chopped
- 2 cloves of garlic, minced
- 1 teaspoon baking powder
- 1 teaspoon ground cumin
- 1 teaspoon sweet paprika
- 1/2 teaspoon salt
- Freshly ground black pepper, to taste
- Handful of fresh parsley, finely chopped
- Water, as needed
- Olive oil, for frying

DIRECTIONS

1. In a large bowl, combine the chickpea flour, baking powder, ground cumin, sweet paprika, salt, black pepper, minced garlic, and finely chopped parsley.
2. Add the chopped onion and shrimp to the bowl, and mix well to coat them with the flour mixture.
3. Gradually add water to the bowl, stirring continuously, until you achieve a thick but pourable batter consistency. The batter should coat the shrimp and onions evenly.
4. Heat a generous amount of olive oil in a frying pan over medium heat.
5. Once the oil is hot, carefully drop spoonfuls of the batter into the pan, forming small fritters. Flatten them slightly with the back of the spoon.
6. Fry the fritters in batches for about 2-3 minutes on each side, or until golden brown and crispy.
7. Use a slotted spoon to transfer the cooked fritters to a plate lined with paper towels to absorb any excess oil.
8. Repeat the frying process with the remaining batter until all the fritters are cooked.
9. Serve the Tortillitas de Camarones hot as a tapa or appetizer, accompanied by a squeeze of fresh lemon juice for an extra burst of flavor.
10. Enjoy the delightful combination of crunchy shrimp fritters and the earthy flavors of chickpea flour, savoring the taste of Andalusia in every bite.

Notes:

1. The key to achieving crispy fritters is to ensure the oil is hot enough before frying. Test the temperature by dropping a small amount of batter into the oil. It should sizzle and bubble immediately.
2. You can customize the seasoning of the batter by adding spices or herbs of your choice, such as cayenne pepper or chopped fresh chilies, to add a hint of heat.
3. Tortillitas de Camarones are best served immediately after frying while they are still warm and crispy.
4. Delight your taste buds with Tortillitas de Camarones, a classic Andalusian dish that showcases the coastal flavors and culinary heritage of the region.

Queso de Cabra con Miel

Queso de Cabra con Miel, or Goat Cheese with Honey, is a simple yet exquisite Spanish dish that beautifully combines the tanginess of goat cheese with the sweetness of honey. This delightful combination of flavors creates a harmonious balance that is both savory and indulgent. Queso de Cabra con Miel is a popular tapa in Spain, often served as an appetizer or part of a cheese platter.

The tradition of pairing goat cheese with honey dates back centuries and can be found in various cuisines around the world. In Spain, the combination of these two ingredients is particularly cherished. The creamy and slightly acidic nature of goat cheese perfectly complements the natural sweetness and smoothness of honey, resulting in a delectable taste experience.

Queso de Cabra con Miel is not only appreciated for its delightful flavors but also for its cultural significance. The dish is a testament to the rich culinary heritage of Spain, where goat cheese has been enjoyed for centuries. The pairing with honey adds an extra layer of sophistication and elevates the flavors of the cheese.

4 SERVINGS | 10 MINUTES | 150 KCAL | EASY

INGREDIENTS

- 200 grams goat cheese, preferably a soft variety
- Honey, to drizzle
- Toasted bread or crackers, for serving
- Fresh rosemary sprigs, for garnish (optional)

DIRECTIONS

1. Remove the goat cheese from its packaging and place it on a serving dish.
2. Use a fork or knife to gently break up the goat cheese into bite-sized pieces, creating a rustic presentation.
3. Drizzle honey generously over the goat cheese, allowing it to cascade down the sides and mingle with the cheese.
4. Garnish the dish with fresh rosemary sprigs, if desired, for an aromatic touch.
5. Serve the Queso de Cabra con Miel alongside toasted bread or crackers, allowing guests to assemble their own bites.
6. Encourage your guests to spread a portion of goat cheese onto a piece of bread or cracker and drizzle additional honey on top for an extra burst of sweetness.
7. Alternatively, you can also serve the goat cheese and honey on a cheese board, accompanied by a selection of fruits, nuts, and cured meats for a more extensive tasting experience.
8. Enjoy the contrasting flavors and textures of tangy goat cheese and silky honey, savoring the richness of this classic Spanish combination.

Notes:

1. Choose a goat cheese that is soft and creamy for a luscious texture. You can also experiment with aged or flavored goat cheeses to add depth to the dish.
2. The amount of honey can be adjusted according to personal preference. Feel free to drizzle as much or as little as desired.
3. Queso de Cabra con Miel can be enjoyed as part of a tapas spread, a cheese platter, or as an accompaniment to a glass of wine or sherry.
4. Indulge in the delightful pairing of Queso de Cabra con Miel, a quintessential Spanish dish that showcases the marriage of creamy goat cheese and sweet honey, providing a taste sensation that is both satisfying and memorable.

TOMATO POWER

Goat cheese is a nutritious choice, rich in essential nutrients. It is a good source of protein, calcium, phosphorus, and vitamin A. Additionally, goat cheese contains lower levels of lactose and cholesterol compared to cow's cheese, making it a suitable option for some individuals with dietary restrictions.

Espinacas con Garbanzos

Espinacas con Garbanzos is a classic Spanish dish that showcases the delightful combination of tender spinach leaves and hearty chickpeas. This vegetarian recipe is packed with flavor and nutrition, making it a popular choice for a satisfying and wholesome meal. With its roots in traditional Spanish cuisine, Espinacas con Garbanzos has been enjoyed for generations as a staple dish, particularly in the region of Andalusia.

The history of Espinacas con Garbanzos can be traced back to the influence of Moorish cuisine in Spain. During the Moorish rule in the Iberian Peninsula, dishes featuring chickpeas and leafy greens like spinach became prevalent. Over time, the dish evolved and incorporated local ingredients and flavors, resulting in the beloved Espinacas con Garbanzos we know today.

4 SERVINGS | **30 MINUTES** | **250 KCAL** | **EASY**

INGREDIENTS

- 500 grams fresh spinach leaves, washed and trimmed
- 400 grams canned chickpeas, drained and rinsed
- 1 onion, finely chopped
- 3 cloves of garlic, minced
- 1 teaspoon ground cumin
- 1 teaspoon sweet paprika
- 1/2 teaspoon ground coriander
- 1/4 teaspoon cayenne pepper (optional, for a hint of spice)
- 2 tablespoons olive oil
- 1 tablespoon tomato paste
- 1 cup vegetable broth
- Salt and pepper, to taste
- Lemon wedges, for serving

DIRECTIONS

1. In a large skillet, heat the olive oil over medium heat. Add the chopped onion and minced garlic, and sauté until they become translucent and fragrant.
2. Stir in the ground cumin, sweet paprika, ground coriander, and cayenne pepper (if using), and cook for an additional minute to toast the spices.
3. Add the tomato paste to the skillet and stir well to coat the onions and garlic.
4. Add the drained chickpeas to the skillet and stir to combine them with the spice mixture.
5. Pour in the vegetable broth and bring the mixture to a simmer. Let it cook for about 5 minutes to allow the flavors to meld together.
6. Gradually add the spinach leaves to the skillet, stirring gently to wilt them. Cook for another 5 minutes, or until the spinach is tender.
7. Season the dish with salt and pepper to taste, adjusting the seasoning according to your preference.
8. Remove the skillet from the heat and let it rest for a few minutes before serving.
9. Serve Espinacas con Garbanzos warm, accompanied by lemon wedges for a refreshing burst of citrus flavor. The dish pairs well with crusty bread or steamed rice.
10. Enjoy the comforting and nourishing combination of spinach and chickpeas, savoring the taste of this traditional Spanish dish that is both satisfying and wholesome.

Notes:

1. Feel free to customize the dish by adding other vegetables or spices according to your taste. Some variations include the addition of roasted red peppers, diced tomatoes, or a sprinkle of smoked paprika.
2. Leftovers of Espinacas con Garbanzos can be refrigerated and reheated the next day, allowing the flavors to further develop.
3. This dish can be enjoyed as a main course for a vegetarian meal or as a side dish to accompany grilled meats or fish.
4. Indulge in the flavors of Spain with Espinacas con Garbanzos, a timeless dish that showcases the simplicity and beauty of traditional Spanish cuisine.

Patatas Bravas

Patatas Bravas, a popular Spanish tapas dish, is a true crowd-pleaser with its crispy fried potatoes and vibrant, spicy tomato sauce. Originating in Madrid, this beloved dish has made its way into the hearts and appetites of people around the world. With its tantalizing combination of textures and flavors, Patatas Bravas is a must-try for any food lover.

The history of Patatas Bravas can be traced back to the early 20th century when potatoes began gaining popularity in Spain. As bars and taverns sought to create enticing appetizers, this iconic dish was born. The name "Bravas" refers to the spicy nature of the tomato sauce, which adds a bold kick to the dish.

To create the perfect Patatas Bravas, start by frying bite-sized potato cubes to a golden crispness. The potatoes should be soft on the inside and delightfully crunchy on the outside. Once fried, they are generously drizzled with a spicy tomato sauce that elevates the dish to new heights.

The spicy tomato sauce is the heart of Patatas Bravas. Made with a base of sautéed onions and garlic, it incorporates aromatic spices like smoked paprika and cayenne pepper for a smoky, fiery flavor.

4 SERVINGS   45 MINUTES   300 KCAL   MED

INGREDIENTS

- 1 kg (2.2 lbs) potatoes, peeled and cut into bite-sized cubes
- Vegetable oil, for frying
- Salt, to taste

For the Spicy Tomato Sauce:
- 2 tablespoons olive oil
- 1 onion, finely chopped
- 3 cloves of garlic, minced
- 1 teaspoon smoked paprika
- 1/2 teaspoon cayenne pepper (adjust to taste)
- 400 grams (14 oz) canned diced tomatoes
- 1 tablespoon tomato paste
- 1 teaspoon sugar
- Salt and pepper, to taste

For the Bravas Sauce:
- 3 tablespoons mayonnaise
- 1 tablespoon ketchup
- 1 teaspoon smoked paprika
- 1/2 teaspoon garlic powder
- 1/2 teaspoon hot sauce (adjust to taste)
- Salt, to taste

DIRECTIONS

1. Heat vegetable oil in a deep frying pan or pot to 180°C (350°F).
2. Carefully add the potato cubes to the hot oil and fry until golden brown and crispy. Remove them from the oil using a slotted spoon and drain on paper towels. Sprinkle with salt while they're still hot.
3. To prepare the spicy tomato sauce, heat olive oil in a saucepan over medium heat. Add the chopped onion and minced garlic, and sauté until softened and fragrant.
4. Stir in the smoked paprika and cayenne pepper, and cook for an additional minute to toast the spices.
5. Add the diced tomatoes, tomato paste, sugar, salt, and pepper to the saucepan. Simmer the sauce for about 15-20 minutes, until it thickens and the flavors meld together. Adjust the seasoning according to your taste.
6. While the sauce is simmering, prepare the bravas sauce. In a small bowl, combine mayonnaise, ketchup, smoked paprika, garlic powder, hot sauce, and salt. Mix well until smooth and creamy. Adjust the seasoning to your preference.
7. Arrange the fried potato cubes on a serving platter. Drizzle the spicy tomato sauce generously over the potatoes.
8. Serve the Patatas Bravas hot, accompanied by the bravas sauce on the side for dipping or drizzling.
9. Enjoy the tantalizing combination of crispy potatoes, zesty tomato sauce, and creamy bravas sauce. The contrast of textures and flavors makes Patatas Bravas a delightful and addictive dish.

Notes:
1. Patatas Bravas can be customized according to your preference. Feel free to adjust the level of spiciness in both the tomato sauce and bravas sauce to suit your taste.
2. Garnish the dish with finely chopped parsley or a sprinkle of smoked paprika for an added touch of color and flavor.
3. This dish is often enjoyed as a tapa or appetizer but can also be served as a side dish to accompany grilled meats or fish.
4. Embrace the vibrant flavors of Spain with Patatas Bravas, a classic and crowd-pleasing dish that captures the essence of Spanish culinary culture.

Tortilla Española

Tortilla Española, also known as Spanish Omelette, is a beloved dish that holds a special place in the hearts of Spaniards. This classic Spanish recipe showcases the simplicity and beauty of a few humble ingredients—eggs, potatoes, onions, and olive oil. With its irresistible combination of flavors and its comforting and satisfying nature, Tortilla Española has become a staple in Spanish households and an iconic dish in Spanish cuisine.

The history of Tortilla Española dates back to the early 19th century. It is believed to have originated in the rural regions of Spain, particularly in the provinces of Extremadura and Castilla. During that time, potatoes were a relatively new ingredient introduced from the Americas, and Spanish cooks began incorporating them into their recipes. The combination of potatoes, onions, and eggs resulted in the birth of Tortilla Española.

Tortilla Española gained popularity across Spain, and its simple yet delicious appeal quickly spread throughout the country. It became a symbol of Spanish culinary tradition and a staple in tapas bars, where it is often served in wedges as a small plate. The dish also made its way onto family dinner tables, enjoyed as a main course accompanied by a fresh salad or crusty bread.

4 SERVINGS | 45 MINUTES | 300 KCAL | EASY

INGREDIENTS

- 4-5 medium-sized potatoes, peeled and thinly sliced
- 1 medium-sized onion, thinly sliced
- 6-8 large eggs
- Salt, to taste
- Olive oil, for frying

DIRECTIONS

1. Heat a generous amount of olive oil in a large non-stick skillet over medium heat.
2. Add the sliced potatoes to the skillet and gently fry them until they are tender but not browned. This process is called "confit," and it ensures that the potatoes will be soft and creamy in the finished tortilla. Remove the potatoes from the skillet and set them aside.
3. In the same skillet, add the sliced onions and sauté until they become translucent and lightly golden. Remove the onions from the skillet and set them aside.
4. In a large mixing bowl, crack the eggs and beat them until well whisked. Season the beaten eggs with salt.
5. Add the fried potatoes and sautéed onions to the beaten eggs. Gently stir to coat the potatoes and onions evenly with the eggs.
6. Heat a small amount of olive oil in the skillet over medium-low heat. Pour the egg, potato, and onion mixture into the skillet, spreading it evenly.
7. Cook the tortilla on one side until the bottom is set and lightly golden. To flip the tortilla, place a flat plate or lid over the skillet, carefully invert the tortilla onto the plate, and then slide it back into the skillet to cook the other side.
8. Continue cooking until the tortilla is set and cooked through. The center should still be slightly runny and moist.
9. Once cooked to your desired consistency, transfer the tortilla to a serving plate and let it cool for a few minutes.
10. Serve the Tortilla Española warm or at room temperature, cut into wedges or squares. It can be enjoyed as a tapa, a main course accompanied by a fresh salad, or as a filling for sandwiches or baguettes.

Notes:

1. Tortilla Española can be customized by adding other ingredients such as cooked vegetables, chorizo, or cheese. Feel free to experiment and make it your own.
2. Leftover Tortilla Española can be refrigerated and enjoyed cold the next day, as it maintains its delicious flavor.

Bacalao a la Vizcaína

Bacalao a la Vizcaína, also known as Basque-style Cod, is a beloved Spanish dish that showcases the rich flavors of salted codfish cooked in a flavorful sauce made from tomatoes, peppers, onions, garlic, and spices. This traditional recipe originates from the Basque Country, a region renowned for its seafood and culinary heritage. With its robust and comforting flavors, Bacalao a la Vizcaína has become a staple in Spanish cuisine, delighting the palates of both locals and visitors.

The history of Bacalao a la Vizcaína dates back centuries, as salted cod has been an essential ingredient in Spanish cuisine since the Middle Ages. The Basque region, with its strong maritime traditions and access to abundant seafood, developed various ways to prepare salted codfish. Bacalao a la Vizcaína emerged as one of the most popular and cherished cod dishes, capturing the essence of Basque gastronomy.

To prepare Bacalao a la Vizcaína, the salted codfish needs to be soaked in water to remove excess salt and rehydrate the flesh.

4 SERVINGS   30 MINUTES   300 KCAL   MED

INGREDIENTS

- 1 pound (450g) salted codfish, soaked and desalted
- 1 large onion, finely chopped
- 3 garlic cloves, minced
- 1 red bell pepper, diced
- 1 green bell pepper, diced
- 2 cups crushed tomatoes
- 1 teaspoon sweet paprika
- 2 bay leaves
- Olive oil
- Salt and pepper to taste
- Fresh parsley, chopped (for garnish)

DIRECTIONS

1. Rinse the soaked codfish under cold water, then place it in a large pot. Cover with water and bring to a boil. Reduce the heat and simmer for about 15 minutes, until the codfish is tender. Remove from the water and let it cool slightly. Remove the skin and bones, and flake the codfish into large chunks.
2. In a large skillet, heat a drizzle of olive oil over medium heat. Add the onions and sauté until translucent. Add the minced garlic and diced bell peppers, and continue cooking for a few minutes until the vegetables soften.
3. Stir in the crushed tomatoes, sweet paprika, and bay leaves. Season with salt and pepper to taste. Simmer the sauce for about 10 minutes, allowing the flavors to meld together.
4. Gently fold in the flaked codfish, ensuring that it is evenly coated with the sauce. Reduce the heat to low and let the mixture simmer for an additional 10 minutes, allowing the flavors to develop.
5. Taste and adjust the seasoning if needed. Remove the bay leaves.
6. Serve the Bacalao a la Vizcaína hot, garnished with a drizzle of olive oil and a sprinkle of fresh parsley. Accompany with crusty bread or white rice.

Notes:

1. Sweet paprika, or pimentón, is a key spice in Spanish cooking. It adds a smoky and slightly sweet flavor to the dish, enhancing the overall taste profile of Bacalao a la Vizcaína.
2. The dish can be enjoyed year-round, but it is particularly popular during Lent, as it does not contain meat. Salted codfish became a popular choice for fasting periods due to its long shelf life and versatility in various recipes.
3. When serving Bacalao a la Vizcaína, you can customize the dish by adding a touch of personal flair. Some variations include adding olives, capers, or a splash of white wine to the sauce for added depth and complexity.
4. The combination of tomatoes, onions, peppers, and garlic in the sauce reflects the Mediterranean influence on Basque cuisine. These ingredients are commonly found in Spanish dishes and contribute to the vibrant and aromatic flavors of Bacalao a la Vizcaína.

BACALAO

Bacalao, or salted codfish, is a nutrient-rich seafood. It is a good source of high-quality protein, low in fat, and rich in omega-3 fatty acids, which are beneficial for heart health. It also provides essential vitamins and minerals, including vitamin D, vitamin B12, and selenium.

Solomillo al Whisky

Solomillo al Whisky, also known as Whiskey-Glazed Pork Tenderloin, is a classic Spanish dish that combines succulent pork tenderloin with a luscious and aromatic whiskey-infused sauce. The dish is a testament to the rich culinary traditions of Spain, where pork is highly valued and celebrated in various regional recipes.

The tender pork tenderloin is the star of this dish, known for its delicate texture and mild flavor. It is seasoned with a sprinkle of salt and black pepper to enhance its natural taste. When cooked to perfection, the pork becomes juicy and tender, creating a satisfying and mouthwatering dining experience.

The whiskey sauce adds a distinctive and indulgent touch to the dish. The combination of whiskey, chicken or beef broth, soy sauce, honey, and Dijon mustard creates a complex flavor profile that balances the sweetness, tanginess, and smoky notes. As the sauce simmers, the flavors meld together, creating a rich and velvety coating for the pork.

Solomillo al Whisky is often served with a garnish of fresh chopped parsley, which adds a touch of freshness and brightness to the dish. The sauce is generously drizzled over the pork, ensuring each bite is infused with the irresistible flavors of the whiskey glaze.

4 SERVINGS | 15 MINUTES | 300 KCAL | MED

INGREDIENTS

- 4 pork tenderloin fillets
- Salt and black pepper to taste
- 2 tablespoons olive oil
- 2 cloves of garlic, minced
- 1/4 cup whiskey
- 1/4 cup chicken or beef broth
- 2 tablespoons soy sauce
- 2 tablespoons honey
- 1 tablespoon Dijon mustard
- Fresh parsley, chopped (for garnish)

DIRECTIONS

1. Season the pork tenderloin fillets with salt and black pepper on both sides.
2. Heat the olive oil in a large skillet over medium-high heat.
3. Add the seasoned pork fillets to the skillet and cook for about 4-5 minutes per side, until browned and cooked through. Remove from the skillet and set aside.
4. In the same skillet, add the minced garlic and cook for about 1 minute until fragrant.
5. Reduce the heat to low and carefully add the whiskey to the skillet. Allow it to simmer for a minute to burn off the alcohol.
6. Add the chicken or beef broth, soy sauce, honey, and Dijon mustard to the skillet. Stir well to combine all the ingredients.
7. Increase the heat to medium and bring the sauce to a gentle simmer. Let it cook for about 2-3 minutes until slightly thickened.
8. Return the pork fillets to the skillet and coat them with the whiskey sauce. Cook for an additional 2-3 minutes, allowing the flavors to meld together.
9. Remove the skillet from the heat and let the pork rest in the sauce for a few minutes.
10. Serve the Solomillo al Whisky on individual plates, drizzling some of the sauce over the pork. Garnish with fresh chopped parsley.
11. This dish pairs well with roasted potatoes or sautéed vegetables.

The Solomillo al Whisky recipe offers a delightful combination of tender pork tenderloin and a luscious whiskey-infused sauce. The whiskey adds depth and complexity to the dish, while the honey and Dijon mustard bring a touch of sweetness and tanginess. It is a dish that embodies the flavors and spirit of Spanish cuisine, showcasing the versatility of pork and the artistry of Spanish cooking techniques. Enjoy this flavorful and aromatic dish with friends and family, and savor the essence of Spanish gastronomy. ¡Buen provecho!

Tarta de Santiago

Tarta de Santiago, also known as Almond Cake of Santiago, is a beloved dessert that originates from the region of Galicia in Spain. This traditional Spanish cake is renowned for its rich almond flavor, moist texture, and symbolic St. James cross decoration. With a history dating back centuries, Tarta de Santiago holds cultural and culinary significance, making it a cherished treat in Spanish cuisine.

Legend has it that Tarta de Santiago was first created as a special offering for pilgrims embarking on the Camino de Santiago, a renowned pilgrimage route leading to the shrine of St. James in Santiago de Compostela. The cake's recipe and distinct cross design became associated with the pilgrimage, symbolizing the journey and devotion of the pilgrims.

The preparation of Tarta de Santiago is relatively simple, but the result is a dessert that is both elegant and deeply satisfying. The key ingredient in this cake is almond flour, which gives it a distinct nutty flavor and moist crumb. Combined with granulated sugar, eggs, and a hint of lemon zest, the cake batter comes together to create a harmonious blend of flavors.

Once baked, the cake is traditionally dusted with powdered sugar and decorated with a St. James cross stencil.

4 SERVINGS | 60 MINUTES | 300 KCAL | MED

INGREDIENTS

- 250 grams almond flour
- 200 grams granulated sugar
- 4 large eggs
- Zest of 1 lemon
- 1 teaspoon ground cinnamon
- Powdered sugar, for dusting

DIRECTIONS

1. Preheat the oven to 180°C (350°F). Grease a round cake pan and line the bottom with parchment paper.
2. In a large mixing bowl, combine the almond flour, granulated sugar, and ground cinnamon. Mix well to ensure the ingredients are evenly distributed.
3. In a separate bowl, beat the eggs until fluffy. Add the lemon zest and continue to beat until well incorporated.
4. Gradually add the beaten eggs to the almond flour mixture, stirring gently to combine. Mix until a smooth batter forms.
5. Pour the batter into the prepared cake pan, smoothing the top with a spatula.
6. Bake in the preheated oven for 30-35 minutes, or until the cake is golden brown and a toothpick inserted into the center comes out clean.
7. Remove the cake from the oven and let it cool in the pan for 10 minutes. Then, transfer it to a wire rack to cool completely.
8. Once the cake has cooled, place a St. James cross stencil on top and dust the cake with powdered sugar. Carefully remove the stencil to reveal the symbol.
9. Serve Tarta de Santiago at room temperature, either on its own or with a dollop of whipped cream or a scoop of vanilla ice cream.
10. Enjoy this emblematic Spanish dessert, savoring the rich almond flavor and the symbolism of the Camino de Santiago that Tarta de Santiago embodies.

Notes:

1. Tarta de Santiago can be stored in an airtight container at room temperature for several days, allowing the flavors to develop and intensify.
2. For an extra touch of authenticity, you can decorate the cake with a small St. James cross made of icing or marzipan.
3. The cake is traditionally gluten-free, making it suitable for those with gluten sensitivities or dietary restrictions.
4. Tarta de Santiago is often enjoyed during special occasions and celebrations in Galicia, serving as a reminder of the cultural and historical significance it holds.